MW00677847

barking up the *family tree*

{kids and their animal kinships}

Mark J. Asher

Andrews McMeel
Publishing

Kansas City

Barking Up the Family Tree copyright © 2005 by Mark J. Asher.
All rights reserved. Printed in China. No part of this book may
be used or reproduced in any manner whatsoever without written
permission except in the case of reprints in the context of reviews. For
information, write Andrews McMeel Publishing, an Andrews McMeel
Universal company, 4520 Main Street, Kansas City, Missouri 64111.

05 06 07 08 09 SDB 10 9 8 7 6 5 4 3 2 1

ISBN-13: 978-0-7407-5459-3
ISBN-10: 0-7407-5459-9

Library of Congress Control Number: 2005921939

Designed by Gayle Chin

ATTENTION: SCHOOLS AND BUSINESSES
Andrews McMeel books are available at quantity discounts with bulk purchase
for educational, business, or sales promotional use. For information, please
write to: Special Sales Department, Andrews McMeel Publishing, 4520 Main
Street, Kansas City, Missouri 64111.

{ there are only three things you need to photograph kids and pets }
patience, perseverance, and prayer

Common Interests { **Wrestling, making a mess.**

What Jake has
learned from Spike { **Don't feed your dog beans!**

What Spike has
learned from Jake { **Whining works!**

If Jake were an
animal, he would be { **A duck, so he could swim, fly, and walk.**

If Spike were a
person, he would be { **A bouncer, so he could patrol the dog park and keep out the lap dogs.**

jake & spike

baylee & nibbles

Common Interests — **Sunflower seeds, nesting in warm spots.**

What Baylee has learned from Nibbles — **How to sleep through loud noises, like a hamster running on her wheel.**

What Nibbles has learned from Baylee — **How to hide from the family dog.**

If Baylee were an animal, she would be — **A rabbit, so people would pick her up and cuddle her.**

If Nibbles were a person, she would be — **A trapeze artist, so she could display her acrobatic skills for a cheering crowd.**

Common Interests { **Splashing in the wading pool, running through the house wet.**

What Blake has learned from Kylee { **To give good hugs and belly rubs.**

What Kylee has learned from Blake { **Following a kid around leads to a lot of good chew toys.**

If Blake were an animal, he would be { **A monkey, so he could hang by his tail and see the world upside down.**

If Kylee were a person, she would be { **A princess, so she could lay in bed and have someone rub her belly and feed her treats.**

blake & kylee

amelia & snowflake

Common Interests **Making people laugh, climbing to high places.**

What Amelia has learned from Snowflake **To calm down from time to time.**

What Snowflake has learned from Amelia **To purr with pride.**

If Amelia were an animal, she would be **A cat, because she likes to play with yarn.**

If Snowflake were a person, she would be **A baker, so she could eat all sorts of goodies.**

Common Interests	**Begging, challenging authority, car rides.**
What Charlie has learned from Mitzi	**When dogs are hungry, hands look like food.**
What Mitzi has learned from Charlie	**Sometimes a young child can mistake a dog for a horse.**
If Charlie were an animal, he would be	**A lion, so everyone would listen to him every time he spoke.**
If Mitzi were a person, she would be	**A track star, so she would receive commercial endorsements for her speed.**

charlie & mitzi

derick & brownie

Common Interests { **Running at full speed, getting dirty.**

What Derick has learned from Brownie { **Dogs have no sweat glands.**

What Brownie has learned from Derick { **Sit, down, and roll over.**

If Derick were an animal, he would be { **A parrot, so he could imitate what other people say.**

If Brownie were a person, he would be { **A top cop who sniffs out the bad guys.**

Common Interests **Long rides at sundown, peanut butter, riding western.**

What Maya has learned from Princess Buttercup **Any secret is safe with her.**

What Princess Buttercup has learned from Mia **How to canter in the right direction.**

If Maya were an animal, she would be **A wild horse, because they can run faster than people and people can't catch them.**

If Princess Buttercup were a person, she would be **A policewoman, so she could be in control.**

maya & princess buttercup

tiera & jake

Common Interests — **Dressing up for Halloween, afternoon snacks.**

What Tiera has learned from Jake — **That a puppy is a girl's best friend.**

What Jake has learned from Tiera — **A kid is not another dog, but a person who demands a lot of their parents' attention.**

If Tiera were an animal, she would be — **A dog, because they get lots of love from everyone.**

If Jake were a person, he would be — **A clown, because he is goofy.**

Common Interests
Climbing, celery sticks with peanut butter, mazes.

What Ali has learned from Checkers
Taking care of a small pet can be a big job.

What Checkers has learned from Ali
The best way to get lots of attention is to be a class pet.

If Ali were an animal, she would be
A horse, so she could ride up mountaintops and watch beautiful sunsets.

If Checkers were a person, he would be
A horse trainer who loves carrots as much as the horses.

ali & checkers

nora & stella

Common Interests { **Singing together—when Nora hits the high notes, Stella howls her little heart out.**

What Nora has learned from Stella { **How to protect her from big birds looking for a little snack.**

What Stella has learned from Nora { **That children can learn to be gentle, loving, and careful with a small pet.**

If Nora were an animal, she would be { **A monkey, so she could explore the forest and find new furry friends.**

If Stella were a person, she would be { **A cafeteria food server, so she could nibble while on the job.**

Common Interests { **Picking on the dog, the top bunk bed.**

What Danial has learned from Grayson { **Cats are good hunters.**

What Grayson has learned from Danial { **Some boys can be kind and gentle.**

If Danial were an animal, he would be { **A panther, because his favorite football team is named after them.**

If Grayson were a person, he would be { **A hunter and explorer like Davy Crockett.**

danial & grayson

tessa & banks

Common Interests { **Being pampered, running with wild abandon.**

What Tessa has learned from Banks { **Dogs listen better than parents do.**

What Banks has learned from Tessa { **How to become top dog in clicker training class.**

If Tessa were an animal, she would be { **A giraffe, so she could see where Mom hides the cookies.**

If Banks were a person, he would be { **A soccer player with Air Bud as a teammate.**

Common Interests **Rearranging their rooms, constantly eating.**

What Venus has learned from Sweetcakes **Bunnies require a lot of care, but give a lot of love in return.**

What Sweetcakes has learned from Venus **When you're cute and cuddly love comes easily.**

If Venus were an animal, she would be **A bunny, so she could play hide and seek all day.**

If Sweetcakes were a person, she would be **A schoolkid, so she wouldn't be penned up all day.**

venus & sweetcakes

jessie & winston

Common Interests	**Playing Man in the Middle, Ding Dongs.**
What Jessie has learned from Winston	**Never trust a dog with your food or drinks.**
What Winston has learned from Jessie	**It's better when a kid feeds you rather than an adult—they serve larger portions!**
If Jessie were an animal, she would be	**A bear, so she could sleep all winter and miss school.**
If Winston were a person, he would be	**A deli owner, so he would always be a short walk from a corned-beef sandwich.**

Common Interests { **Strolls through the neighborhood, climbing big rocks.**

What Emile has learned from Billy { **When he bleats, he wants to eat or play.**

What Billy has learned from Emile { **How to heel.**

If Emile were an animal, he would be { **A jaguar, because they are big and fast.**

If Billy were a person, he would be { **A gardener, so he could mow lawns and prune roses.**

emile & billy

evan & ivory

Common Interests **{** **Getting rewarded for good behavior, junk food, back rubs.**

What Evan has learned from Ivory **{** **Dogs expect treats for tricks.**

What Ivory has learned from Evan **{** **Kids are more likely to give free handouts than adults.**

If Evan were an animal, he would be **{** **A dog, because they don't have to go to school!**

If Ivory were a person, he would be **{** **Evan, because he gets three meals a day plus dessert!**

Common Interests **{ Barrel racing, carrots, long trails.**

What Dani Sue has
learned from Cody **{ The responsibility of taking care
of a 1,200-pound animal.**

What Cody has learned
from Dani Sue **{ Appreciate today—your owner won't
stay young and light forever.**

If Dani Sue were an
animal, she would be **{ A dolphin, because they swim fast and
have a humongous playground.**

If Cody were a
person, he would be **{ A food taster, so he would be paid for
his passion instead of scorned.**

dani sue & cody

wynn & ruby

Common Interests	**Playing in the mud puddles, digging holes in the garden.**
What Wynn has learned from Ruby	**How to get the best seat in the van on road trips.**
What Ruby has learned from Wynn	**How to worm their way into Mom's bedroom.**
If Wynn were an animal, he would be	**A lion, because he would get to eat other animals and not be eaten.**
If Ruby were a person, she would be	**A cowboy, because she likes chasing cows.**

Common Interests	**Being a big sister and dealing with tagalongs, tuna fish.**
What Katie has learned from Missy	**Sleeping in is the best part of the day.**
What Missy has learned from Katie	**Nothing, for a cat knows it all!**
If Katie were an animal, she would be	**A dolphin, because they are intelligent, work well with others, and like to play.**
If Missy were a person, she would be	**A princess that does nothing but sit around and look pretty.**

katie & missy

jade & harley

Common Interests { **Fancy shoes—Jade likes to wear them; Harley likes to eat them.**

What Jade has learned from Harley { **To loosen up, get dirty, and go wild.**

What Harley has learned from Jade { **A bath is a good thing if you want to be let in the house.**

If Jade were an animal, she would be { **A horse, so she could look pretty with ribbons in her mane.**

If Harley were a person, he would be { **An everyday average guy who likes to stay home, eat, and watch TV.**

Common Interests { **Mice—Jack likes to play with them; Freddy likes to eat them.**

What Jack has learned from Freddy { **That snakes have whiskers!**

What Freddy has learned from Jack { **Kids whisper one thing to their pet snakes and tell their parents another.**

If Jack were an animal, he would be { **An octopus, so he could do his homework and play caroms at the same time.**

If Freddy were a person, he would be { **A pet store worker. When no one was looking, he would eat all the mice.**

jack & freddy

kimberly & jake

Common Interests	**Swimming in the ocean; sharing a big, stuffy pillow.**
What Kimberly has learned from Jake	**How to love and care for him as he gets older.**
What Jake has learned from Kimberly	**How to shake hands.**
If Kimberly were an animal, she would be	**A dog, because they don't have to do anything!**
If Jake were a person, he would be	**Jake is a person—he is Kimberly's older brother!**

Common Interests { **Being loud, getting cozy with Mom.**

What Riley has learned from Houdini { **Not to mess with him.**

What Houdini has learned from Riley { **To be gentle with babies.**

If Riley were an animal, he would be { **A snake, because they are rare and cool.**

If Houdini were a person, he would be { **Riley, to get more of Mom's affection.**

riley & houdini

atticus & possum

Common Interests **Chasing lizards, lounging.**

What Atticus has learned from Possum **How to bark.**

What Possum has learned from Atticus **How to be pulled in a red wagon and act like he's having fun.**

If Atticus were an animal, he would be **Possum, because she gets to run around without getting yelled at.**

If Possum were a person, she would be **A nurse, so she could care for people.**

Common Interests **Flowers—Catherine loves the way they smell; Sparkle likes the way they taste.**

What Catherine has learned from Sparkle **How to love and care for him.**

What Sparkle has learned from Catherine **How to eat his food without standing in it.**

If Catherine were an animal, she would be **A wild stallion, because they are fast and free.**

If Sparkle were a person, he would be **A bossy little tyrant with bad table manners.**

catherine & sparkle

jordan & jessie

Common Interests { **Camping outdoors, dog-paddling in the river, eating sweets.**

What Jordan has learned from Jessie { **Not to leave his toys on the floor, especially stuffed animals.**

What Jessie has learned from Jordan { **If she waits until the adults go to bed she can sleep on Jordan's bed.**

If Jordan were an animal, he would be { **A cheetah, because they are strong and fast.**

If Jessie were a person, she would be { **An opera singer, because she loves to hear her own voice.**

Common Interests { **Sticking their tongues out, keeping secrets.**

What Ariel has learned from Sioux { **The importance of following safety rules.**

What Sioux has learned from Ariel { **How to improve her trotting and backing skills.**

If Ariel were an animal, she would be { **A mustang, because they get to gallop freely and race eagles.**

If Sioux were a person, she would be { **An actor, because she likes to perform in front of others.**

ariel & sioux

robbie & hershey

Common Interests { **Pillow talk, popcorn.**

What Robbie has learned from Hershey { **To stay out of the way when he is fetching a ball.**

What Hershey has learned from Robbie { **How to have fun with shaving cream in the bathtub.**

If Robbie were an animal, he would be { **A reindeer, so he could help Santa's sled fly.**

If Hershey were a person, he would be { **A water polo player, so he could enjoy his favorite things—water, swimming, and balls.**

Common Interests ⎰ **Climbing trees, afternoon naps.**

What McKayla has
learned from Toby ⎰ **How to look cute and get attention.**

What Toby has learned
from McKayla ⎰ **Sometimes you've got to meow
loudly to get what you want.**

If McKayla were an
animal, she would be ⎰ **A kitten, so she could curl up on
the couch without being asked
about her homework.**

If Toby were a person,
he would be ⎰ **A famous country singer, so all the
girls would swoon over him.**

mckayla & toby

cy & kyia

Common Interests { **Playing superheroes, digging for bones—Cy for dinosaur bones; Kyia for any bones.**

What Cy has learned from Kyia { **To walk in a circle three times before lying down.**

What Kyia has learned from Cy { **There's no good reason to sit when you can play.**

If Cy were an animal, he would be { **A Tyrannosaurus Rex, because he is the king of all dinosaurs.**

If Kyia were a person, she would be { **A restless teenager one minute; the queen of England the next.**

Common Interests { **Backyard adventures, digging for buried treasures.**

What Allison has learned from Andy { **Your dog will give you licks whether you're happy or sad.**

What Andy has learned from Allison { **Always respect your owner, because you might get a treat.**

If Allison were an animal, she would be { **A dog, because they never have to worry about getting their clothes dirty.**

If Andy were a person, he would be { **A trashman, because people throw away good stuff.**

allison & andy

mia & buttercup

Common Interests { **Chomping carrots loudly, strolling with the bunny in the baby carriage.**

What Mia has learned from Buttercup { **To be nicer to her animals.**

What Buttercup has learned from Mia { **Even when he nips Mia, she still loves him.**

If Mia were an animal, she would be { **One of her aunt Laurie's pets, because then she would be spoiled rotten!**

If Buttercup were a person, he would be { **Jester, the family's chocolate Lab— he gets more to eat.**

Common Interests **{ Playing tag, watching *Air Bud*.**

What Jake has
learned from Kona **{ How to run fast and stop quick.**

What Kona has
learned from Jake **{ How to play hide and seek.**

If Jake were an
animal, he would be **{ A giraffe, so he could be taller than his dad.**

If Kona were a
person, he would be **{ A kid, so he could go to school with Jake.**

jake & kona

patrick & honey

Common Interests { **Riding around the neighborhood in the horse carriage, house parties.**

What Patrick has learned from Honey { **Be careful where you step!**

What Honey has learned from Patrick { **How to deal with motorcycles, skateboards, and bikes whizzing through the barn.**

If Patrick were an animal, he would be { **A miniature schnauzer with never-ending energy.**

If Honey were a person, she would be { **A fairy-tale princess who is loved and doted on by all.**

Common Interests { **Bouncing balls, watching cartoons.**

What Anna has learned from Maggie { **To be peaceful.**

What Maggie has learned from Anna { **To be playful.**

If Anna were an animal, she would be { **A dog that barks and plays all of the time.**

If Maggie were a person, she would be { **A quiet little girl that is sweet and gentle.**

anna & maggie

ethan & mo

Common Interests { **Playing chase, doughnuts.**

What Ethan has learned from Mo { **Not to be wild and crazy all the time.**

What Mo has learned from Ethan { **Being brushed can calm you down.**

If Ethan were an animal, he would be { **A dog, because they don't have to clean up their messes.**

If Mo were a person, he would be { **An NFL running back with a great cutback move.**

Common Interests { **Needing attention from Mom, jumping on the furniture.**

What Olivia has learned from Samantha { **Cats do not like dogs as much as dogs like cats.**

What Samantha has learned from Olivia { **To go only in the litter box or there will be one cranky cat owner.**

If Olivia were an animal, she would be { **A dolphin, because they're smart and fast and never get cold in the water.**

If Samantha were a person, she would be { **A hermit that reads mystery novels all day long.**

olivia & samantha

ACKNOWLEDGEMENTS

When you're a kid, the last thing you want to do is spend part of your day complying with a photographer's wishes. A huge thanks to those who participated in this book, slowing down just long enough for me to capture them with their equally exuberant four-legged friends. Your spontaneity, silliness, and innocence certainly brought out the kid in me! As well, I owe a tremendous debt of gratitude to the parents who cajoled, bribed, pleaded, reasoned, begged, and ultimately convinced their children that sitting still for a few minutes, for a book (and for my physical and mental health), was a priority over everything else that popped into their heads.

To all at Andrews McMeel for believing in me and helping to make my first book with them a smooth and rewarding experience: Patty Rice, Jennifer Fox, Joshua Brewster, and John Carroll.

To those who offered their invaluable resources: Nancy and Evan Archerd, Jennifer McMahon, Sandra Schatz, Rob Fox, Fabian Gonzalez, and Matt Moore (aka the Pumpkin Man) at Pierson Cattle and Hay.

Special thanks to Gayle Chin, for another brilliant job of complementing my photography with great design; Marin Filmworks; Kari Gies at the North Mountain Nature Center in Ashland, Oregon; and the rottweiler puppy who magically appeared and grabbed Kyia's attention.

{ to Humphrey, for leading me here }

{there is no better companion, teacher, or medicine for a child than the family pet}
~anonymous~